AN EMPTY CRADLE,

A FULL HEART

Christine O'Keeffe Lafser
Foreword by Phyllis Tickle

AN EMPTY CRADLE
A Full Heart

*Reflections for
mothers and fathers
after miscarriage, stillbirth,
or infant death*

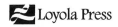

Loyola Press

Chicago

Loyola Press

3441 North Ashland Avenue
Chicago, Illinois 60657

Interior design by Lisa Buckley

Library of Congress Cataloging-in-Publication Data
Lafser, Christine O'Keeffe.
    An empty cradle, a full heart: reflections for mothers and fathers
after miscarriage, stillbirth, or infant death/Christine O'Keeffe Lafser;
foreword by Phyllis Tickle.
       p.   cm.
    Includes bibliographical references.
    ISBN 0-8294-1173-9
    1. Parents — Prayer-books and devotions — English. 2. Bereavement —
Religious aspects — Christianity — Meditations. 3. Infants (Newborn) —
Death — Religious aspects — Christianity — Meditations. 4. Fetal death —
Religious aspects — Christianity — Meditations. I. Title.
BV4907.L34 1998
242'.4 — dc21   98-15190
                                                                      CIP

Printed in the United States of America
98 99 00 01 02 / 10 9 8 7 6 5 4 3 2 1

Dedicated to all the babies our arms ache to hold.

For Bobby and Jenny,
and for Luke,
who made this book possible.

We Americans have never quite reached consensus about when — at what exact moment in time — a baby becomes a baby. Perhaps our country will never be comforted by any commonality — legal or political — of agreement. But psychologically and emotionally the matter is fairly clear for most of us; experientially it is terribly, terribly clear for those of us who have lost our children to pre-, peri-, or neonatal death.

It seems to me, as one in that sad group of many, that a child "becomes" as soon as it begins to leave some impress upon the being of another person. For some people, that can mean that a child *is* as soon as his or her parents begin to yearn toward his or her beginning. For most of us who have walked the long miles of love that lead to parenthood, however, a child *is* when the first suspicion of pregnancy appears — the first missed period, the first queasiness, the first tenderness in one's breasts. From that moment of recognition on, the thing-in-process is no longer "thing" but "baby" — our baby, my baby, the baby — but by whatever name, still a baby, a human being for those blessed few who are privy to the secret.

The secret is a baby, in other words, because he or she has just begun to make a difference in other human beings' lives; because he or she is now a stimulus to other people, a stimulus that demands reaction and will receive it whether or no; because for most parents-to-be, their very identity to themselves and to each other has been redefined forever by that thing-turned-baby.

But sometimes for some of us — far too often for a few of us — parenting is like a bowl of mixed winter bulbs set on a windowsill to bloom after Christmas. Life stirs within the warming humus. The narcissus spears emerge and spike in their thrusting, defiant praise to spring, and those who see their paean in green and white are sustained and cheered. But the narcissus and the gardener know that waiting below in the moist nest of their beginning are the bulbs of the far shorter and more deeply colorful grape hyacinth, and they too have begun to stir.

The narcissus know because they themselves are rooted where the hyacinths' tentative, fingering rootlets are reaching out for more sustenance. The narcissus know because their own roots, even their very bulbs, are being gently pushed into different positions. The narcissus know because the gardener seems more attentive, more watchful, more present, turning the bowl a bit, adding water here and light there. If it were not too romantic a stretch, we might even say that the narcissus are happy.

In fact, we probably must say the narcissus are happy in their windowsill bowl, because we are also going to have to account for what they are when the hyacinth bulbs sigh a little sigh beneath their humus blanket, give one small shake, and then cease to be.

Within days their small hyacinth rootlets have retreated, and their tiny little bulbous hyacinth bodies have begun returning to the humus which had been their nurture. The homeowners may say, "How sad that the hyacinths don't seem to be coming up after all," but it is nothing to them that the hyacinths have failed this late winter. There is always next year after Christmas, and besides, since the hyacinths never came, it is hard to regret their absence.

The hyacinths weren't ever there, you see, except for the narcissus who feel now, continuously, the emptying of their space and the cooling of the humus. Oh, they will go on blooming, of course; they will continue to spike and even to give off their sweet fragrance to the surrounding air. But they will know. The narcissus will know that they are paler than the gardener had intended, and all for lack of the rich royal blues that were to be their contrast. When their thrust-ing spikes finally overreach themselves and begin to tumble, the narcissus know that there will be no border of young life to shield their going or to give purpose to the indoor garden. And in a room that lacks the rich odors of birthing soil and ongoing life, the narcissus will even come in time to find their own fragrance strangely cloying. The narcissus will know all these things for the rest of their time in the window bowl garden, because for them the hyacinths were real. But it is not so for those who simply pass the windowsill. For them there are not and never were any hyacinths.

If those who stop to have a sandwich in front of the winter bowl or to glance out into the yard beyond the window, or who merely go by on their busy way toward some household chore — if those passersby feel no grief for the hyacinths, they are to be understood perhaps; but for me and for Christine O'Keeffe Lafser and for millions like us, they are no longer to be so easily excused.

The problem with pre-, peri-, and neonatal death is that, like the passing of the hyacinths, it occurs below the surface and sight lines of life. The life it takes occurs in too small and confined a space to stimulate beyond its own intimate environs. The death is never there because the life was never recognized . . . never, that is, except to the narcissus, never except to the few who shared the bowl on the windowsill. *An Empty Cradle, A Full Heart* is the mourning song of the narcissus.

Gentle at times, assertive and faithfully angry at others, but always informed by frankness of emotion and the candor of a deeply wounded heart, this small volume ranges quietly and beautifully over the whole of what Lafser calls "the nebulous death." Intended to comfort, counsel, and affirm both mothers and fathers, the book is also a clarion call to the church: It is time, liturgically and pastorally, to celebrate the reality of life agonizingly lost before or during birth with a fervor equal to that with which we acknowledge the reality of life willfully ended during the same period.

And Lafser's words are for the passersby as well, for those not-unkind familiars of the house who presently can glance at the incomplete bowl of bulbs and still move carelessly on. As its title suggests, *An Empty Cradle* is a textbook of the heart. It is, for the willing, an instruction in how to feel with the understanding and in how to exercise informed compassion with one's actions and words. Pray God that few will need such comfort and/or instruction, but those who do will most surely find both of them here.

—PHYLLIS TICKLE

W hen my babies died,
I didn't think I would ever be happy again.

Bereavement after the loss of a baby is often
quiet and lonely, because we have no vehicle for its
expression. There is no wake or funeral, no grave site,
no memorial to our baby's life or death. There are
often no photographs or favorite toys, no little clothes
to remind us of just how tiny he or she was. For many
of us, even the sex of our baby is unknown.

Often the people around us can't seem to understand how it could hurt so badly to lose a baby they think
we didn't really know. Since there are no real memories
of our little one's life, they have a hard time compre-
hending the depth of our love and grief. Though they
don't mean to hurt us with their attitudes and com-
ments, sometimes their words of comfort sound cruel.

I offer these short reflections to assure you that
what you are feeling is common to parents who have

xv ~

lost a child through miscarriage, stillbirth, or infant death, and to give you hope, encouragement, and support as you grieve. Many are based on my own experiences after the deaths of my children; others reflect the experiences of family members and friends whose children have died. Though written primarily for mothers and fathers, they are also appropriate for siblings, grandparents, aunts and uncles, friends and neighbors, and all who mourn the loss of a little baby. Doctors, nurses, pastors, and counselors may also find in these pages the insight needed to better understand, minister to, and help those who grieve.

The grief process does not proceed in a straight line from despair to hope. Some days will be unbearable; some will be much better. This is the nature of grief. I can't encourage you enough to allow yourself to grieve in your own way, at your own pace — and to use this book in whatever way helps you most.

You may find that on some days, especially right after your baby's death, you may not be able to read it at all. If it hurts too much, put it down for a few days and try again another time. Later you may find that picking it up and thumbing through it, reading reflections here and there, may be most helpful.

Some people stop on a page that expresses just how they feel that day, finding comfort in knowing that other grieving parents have shared their feelings. Others use the book to help them move on by reading until they find a passage that offers hope for tomorrow. Still others have told me that, when they were ready, they read the book from front to back, blinking back their tears. And some reread sections as they needed them, either to help them get through the rough days or to rejoice and thank God on good days.

Different reflections will be helpful on different days and at different times. Some days you may find a passage that expresses exactly how you feel; other days a completely different sentiment will speak to your heart. Sharing these passages with the people you love is a good way to help them understand what you are going through. Being able to share our grief with each other, and to talk about the many feelings that accompanied that grief, united me and my husband in a whole new way after our babies died.

Above all, I urge you to pay particular attention to the Scripture verses, for it is in them that I think you will find real consolation.

For, finally, the healing comes. A friend once told me this book reminded him of a collection of psalms of lament and praise, with the psalm of lament always bringing one back to faith. As time passed, I found I had been strengthened by pain, like gold tried in the fire. That is what I desire for you: that this book will help bring you to God in a new way, strengthening and renewing your faith, even in the face of such deep sorrow.

I hope it will console you to remember that God loves each of us the way we love our own children. It helps some parents to think of God holding their baby tenderly for them. I think he wants to hold us, too, as we grieve. We need only to turn to his embrace.

—CHRISTINE O'KEEFFE LAFSER

~ REFLECTIONS

FOR MOTHERS

I sit in the rocking chair, pretending to rock the baby whose heart beat for too short a time. Last week I rocked him while he was still inside me. I thought of how he would feel in my arms and looked forward to stroking his face and kissing his neck. I talked to him and made plans for him. I read to him and sang to him.

~ 4

But now he is gone. I have to trust that the Lord is holding him, and that angels are singing to him now. Yet I still can't quite give him up, so I sit and pretend to rock him. I have tried to sing to him, but I can't. I know God can read my heart. He knows my sadness and he understands.

Can a woman forget her infant,

be without tenderness for the child of her womb?

ISAIAH 49:15 *(NAB)*

5 ~

When he didn't hear
a heartbeat, the obstetrician ordered an ultrasound.
There was a long wait while I drank what seemed
to be gallons of water. The ultrasound technologist
didn't speak except for curt instructions, and the
monitor was turned away from me so that I couldn't

see the image of my baby. When I asked a question,
she made it clear that I shouldn't interrupt her work.

The radiologist came in a little while later,
conferred briefly with the technologist, and studied
the monitor. She told me that she could not detect
a heartbeat and that my baby was probably dead.
Then she was gone, leaving me scared, shocked, and
all alone.

Why didn't they talk to me? Why didn't they
let me see my baby on the screen? Why were they
so anxious to get me out of there?

*Be gracious to me, O L*ORD*, for I am languishing;*

   *O L*ORD*, heal me, for my bones are shaking*

      with terror.

My soul also is struck with terror,

   *while you, O L*ORD *— how long?*

7 ~

PSALM 6:2-3

*T*here was a lot of blood
and a lot of pain. A miscarriage. There had been
no heartbeat on the ultrasound.

"We need to do a D&C now," the doctor said.

I remember waking up in the recovery room.
The nurse said my name.

~ 8

"Is it over?" I asked.

She nodded. Only then did I lose hope.
Only then did I know that my baby was really dead.

Come to me, all you that are weary and are carrying heavy burdens, and I will give you rest.

MATTHEW 11:28

9 ~

My son doesn't understand my silence or my tears. He doesn't know why I want to hold him and rock him for so long. He is too little to understand that his baby brother has died and won't be coming home.

I need to hold this little child to convince myself of the reality of his sweet flesh; yes, he really is here and he is mine. I still have one precious child.

He tolerates my hugs for as long as a toddler can, then scampers away to play. He is a delight and makes me smile in spite of my grief. He comforts me with his exuberance. He brings me out of myself because he needs a whole and happy mother too. I am trying. Please help me, Lord, to put aside my grief and rejoice in the life of my dear son.

Great are the works of the LORD,

*   to be treasured for all their delights.*

PSALM 111:2 *(NAB)*

My breasts are still full and heavy. I still feel tired. It's as if my body doesn't know that I'm no longer pregnant. What a cruel joke — even my body was fooled. When will the truth catch up with me, and what will I do when all of me knows that my baby is dead?

I cry to you and you do not answer me;

I stand, and you merely look at me.

You have turned cruel to me;

with the might of your hand you persecute me.

JOB 30:20—21   13 ~

$\sim$ 14

Υesterday I ran into
an old neighbor in the grocery store. She asked
when the baby was due. I told her that the baby
had died, and that the contractions should begin
in the next few days. Her face reflected her horror
and compassion. She didn't know what to say.
Neither did I. She patted my hand as she left and
said she would pray for me. I didn't cry. Part of
me still feels numb.

These days of waiting for the contractions
to begin are very bad. Anticipation of delivery
should be joyous, not sad.

The joy of our hearts has ceased;

    our dancing has been turned to mourning.

LAMENTATIONS 5:15

*E*verything makes me cry. Today, three television commercials made me cry. When the mail came, the discount-store catalog made me cry. In the grocery store, I had to avoid the baby-care aisle altogether. Anything will do it: a song, a phrase, a Scripture passage, a reference to the past or the future. Even the calendar brings tears to my eyes.

~ 16

I feel so silly, but I can't help it. I try not to cry, but the tears come unbidden, and at the oddest times. I'm getting a little better at blinking them back, but the lump in my throat gets bigger and bigger.

My eyes will flow without ceasing,

without respite.

LAMENTATIONS 3:49

17 ~

MOTHERS

I am afraid I am going to die. I have never feared death before, but now it is a very real fear. I think of how my family would cope without me. My husband needs me. My other children need me. I have more living to do.

Why do I feel like an egg with tiny cracks in the shell — so fragile, so shattered, so weak? What if my husband dies instead? I have this terrible feeling that something horrible is going to happen to us again.

They cried out in fear. But immediately Jesus
spoke to them and said, "Take heart, it is I;
do not be afraid."

MATTHEW 14:26–27

MOTHERS

I thought he was taking a long nap. We'd had a busy day, and it didn't seem strange for him to be sleeping a little longer than usual. After a while, I went upstairs to check on him. He was lying peacefully in his crib, but he was dead. I can't forget the horror of that moment.

I keep remembering the way he looked when I found him. Could I have saved him if I had checked on him sooner?

And after you have suffered for a little while, the God of all grace, who has called you to his eternal glory in Christ, will himself restore, support, strengthen, and establish you.

1 PETER 5:10

21 ~

A friend came over today and insisted I go out with her. She didn't try to make me forget — how could I? — but we still had fun. We even laughed a couple of times. We cried too. I didn't think I would be able to talk so freely, but her willingness to listen made it easy, and I felt better.

Faithful friends are beyond price;

   no amount can balance their worth.
Faithful friends are life-saving medicine.

SIRACH 6:15—16

My list of things to do has become much smaller. I don't have to wash the hand-me-down baby clothes or finish the nursery or decide which kind of car seat to buy. I don't have to find a rocking chair or decide what diapers to use. I don't have to pick out a baby monitor or make arrangements for day care. I don't have to decide whether to go back to work — there is no baby to stay home with. I don't have to look through those baby name books or read all that stuff the obstetrician gave me. I don't have to interview pediatricians.

All those decisions and tasks that once seemed so overwhelming are gone now. I have nothing to do but cry. Now I see that none of that was really important. What was important is gone. I miss you, my baby.

You are worried and distracted by many things;

there is need of only one thing.

LUKE 10:41—42

I don't know what to do with the half-finished Noah's ark quilt. I can't finish it, but I can't throw it away either. It was for my baby. I can't bear that she will never sleep under it. Maybe someday I'll know how to deal with it, but for now I don't know what to do.

*Blessed are those who mourn, for they will
be comforted.*

MATTHEW 5:4

I feel empty, so I eat.
Nothing I eat satisfies me, so I eat something else.
But that doesn't help either. After a while I feel
bloated, not satisfied. Why do I keep trying to fill
this emptiness with food when I know it doesn't
work? I'm gaining weight, and I feel fat and
unattractive. I tell myself that I would be gaining
weight if I were still pregnant, but I know it's
not the same. Eating is just something I do. It
fills the time.

~ 28

My soul thirsts for God,

for the living God.

When shall I come and behold

the face of God?

PSALM 42:2

All I've ever wanted
to be is a wife and mother. Even in kindergarten,
I drew little houses with lots of children inside.
I'm great with kids.

What do you want from me, God? Why did
you give me such desire and so many talents and
then deny me children? I want to do your will, but
can't I be a mommy too?

~ 30

How often have I desired to gather your children

together as a hen gathers her brood under her wings.

LUKE 13:34

*T*oday is Mother's Day.
I don't know where I stand. Am I a mother if my
baby doesn't live? I've never raised a child or
even brought one home from the hospital. The
closest I have come is loving the baby I carried
under my heart. Am I a mother?

Turn to me and be gracious to me,
for I am lonely and afflicted.
Relieve the troubles of my heart,
and bring me out of my distress.

PSALM 25:16—17

I can find no peace. My baby is dead. I will not feed him or see him take his first steps. He won't wipe off my kisses and say, "Oh, Mom!" He won't play catch with his dad or jump in mud puddles. He won't hear a bedtime story or ride a bicycle. I can find no peace. My baby is dead.

A voice is heard in Ramah,

lamentation and bitter weeping.

Rachel is weeping for her children;

she refuses to be comforted for her children,

because they are no more.

35 ~

JEREMIAH 31:15

I am amazed by the number of women who quietly tell me of their own lost child. I never knew they, too, have shared this sadness. I have known some of these women all my life, and still I never knew. It is as if we are part of a secret sorority none of us knew existed. They give me hope and courage. They have each lived through this horror. I can too.

I have no silver or gold, but what I have I give you.

ACTS 3:6

I try to stay busy. I've made slipcovers and new curtains for the living room. I've stripped and waxed the hardwood floors. I've cleaned out the closets (except for the one in the room that was going to be the baby's), and I'm thinking about pulling up the kitchen floor and putting down new tile. What will I do when I run out of projects?

~ 38

Do not worry about tomorrow; tomorrow will take care of itself. Sufficient for a day is its own evil.

MATTHEW 6:34 *(NAB)*

I am so desperate that
I bargain with God.

*Please take this knowledge away from me and let it be
a nightmare. Please make my baby alive and whole again. Please
give me a baby who will live. I will do anything. I will be good
the rest of my life. I will raise my children to give you honor and
glory and to love you with all their hearts. They will be examples
of goodness and kindness and will always obey you. I will give
up all my possessions. I will love you forever, if only you will take
this pain away and give me my baby, Lord.*

I feel ashamed for wanting to bargain with
God, but I can't help it. I don't know what else
to do. Only God can make it better.

In her bitterness she prayed to the LORD, weeping copiously, and she made a vow, promising:
"O LORD of hosts, if you look with pity on the misery of your handmaid, if you remember me and do not forget me, if you give your handmaid a male child, I will give him to the LORD for as long as he lives."

1 SAMUEL 1:10–11 (*NAB*)

*H*er little boy was eight months old when he died of a rare heart condition. She was a nurse, and she knew the pain he was in at the end. How could she watch her little boy suffer so?

Then she thought of Mary standing at the foot of the cross. "If Mary could do that, I can do this," she said, and it gave her strength.

I marvel at her faith as she recounts those last days. Help me to be strong too, Lord.

No trial has come to you but what is human. God is faithful and will not let you be tried beyond your strength; but with the trial he will also provide a way out, so that you may be able to bear it.

1 CORINTHIANS 10:13 *(NAB)*

I forgot about it for a
while today. It was a nice afternoon, and some
of us decided to eat our lunches outside. The sun
felt warm on my face, and the birds were singing.
We walked briskly around the block and acted a
little silly. I felt so good and free and blessed by
the beautiful day that I almost started singing.
Of course I remembered again later, but what
a welcome reprieve that lunch was.

The people who walked in darkness
    have seen a great light;
those who lived in a land of deep darkness —
    on them light has shined.

45 ~

*I*t seems as if the whole world is pregnant. Everywhere I go I see pregnant women. I am ashamed to admit that I am avoiding my mother's next-door neighbor. Her baby is due a week after our child was. I just can't look at her right now. I feel so unkind, but every time I see her I feel jealous, resentful, or so sad that I start to cry.

In those days Mary set out and went with haste to
a Judean town in the hill country, where she entered
the house of Zechariah and greeted Elizabeth.
When Elizabeth heard Mary's greeting, the child
leaped in her womb. And Elizabeth was filled
with the Holy Spirit and exclaimed with a loud cry,
"Blessed are you among women, and blessed is the
fruit of your womb."

LUKE 1:39—42

I look at the maternity clothes and know I should pack them away. But I can't. They weren't supposed to be put away until August, and I just can't do it in May. I didn't wear them long enough.

Suddenly I hate all of my summer clothes.

~ 48

Why do you worry about clothing? Consider the
lilies of the field, how they grow; they neither
toil nor spin, yet I tell you, even Solomon in all
his glory was not clothed like one of these.

MATTHEW 6:28–29

*H*ow anxious I was for the pregnancy to be over. How impatient I was for each day to pass. Little did I know that those were the only days I would have with you. Why did I wish them away instead of savoring each moment we had together?

~ 50

Teach us to count our days

  that we may gain a wise heart.

PSALM 90:12

I was starting to get excited about the baby just before we lost her. At first, I wasn't too sure. I was a little disappointed when the pregnancy test was positive. I felt scared and unprepared.

Maybe I didn't love her enough. Maybe my body rejected her because my mind and heart weren't ready. Maybe there is some sort of biochemical-feedback system that scientists haven't discovered yet.

I know it sounds silly, but I feel so guilty. I'm sorry if I did something wrong, or if I didn't love you enough. I do love you. I wish you were here. I hope I didn't make you die.

Just as you do not know how the breath comes to the bones in the mother's womb, so you do not know the work of God.

ECCLESIASTES 11:5

I'm not interested in food anymore. It doesn't taste good, and it takes too much energy to fix. I'm losing weight — I can tell by my clothes. The pants I wore before I was pregnant are loose around my waist. I want to stay healthy, so I make myself eat. But it is hard.

~ 54

Therefore, we are not discouraged; rather,

although our outer self is wasting away,

our inner self is being renewed day by day.

2 CORINTHIANS 4:16 *(NAB)*

My sister looks at
me with kindness and listens. She holds me, and
we cry together. With her I can let go and sob.
Then, when our tears are spent, she says something
that makes us both laugh. I find comfort in her
arms, if only for a little while.

~ 56

A friend loves at all times,

    and kinfolk are born to share adversity.

PROVERBS 17:17

57 ~

I feel so alone. We weren't even sure I was pregnant when my husband's unit was deployed, and now I've lost the baby. I have no way to let him know what has happened. What if he doesn't come home? What if the war takes him from me too?

I wish he were here to hold me and grieve with me. I miss him. My other children are so little. I am grateful to have them, but my heart still aches for my dead baby. I need an adult to talk to, and my husband to hold.

How long, O LORD? Will you forget me forever?
  How long will you hide your face from me?
How long must I bear pain in my soul,
  and have sorrow in my heart all day long?

PSALM 13:1—2

*O*ur car broke down on the way home from the zoo. After waiting four hours in the repair shop, we stood in line to pay for the parts. The cashiers were talking among themselves as if we weren't there. We stood in line as they laughed about their abortions.

~ 60

How could they be so cavalier about killing their babies when my heart was broken because my precious little ones died? Why couldn't I have them? Give me all the babies. I will love them and care for them.

Do not judge, so that you may not be judged.
For with the judgment you make you will
be judged, and the measure you give will be
the measure you get.

MATTHEW 7:1–2

I know my self-worth doesn't stem from my ability to have children. But I have always wanted children and just assumed that I would have them when the time and circumstances were right.

Why, God? Why did you take my baby from me? Why am I unable to have a healthy child or a child who can live to be born? I've never felt so defective and inadequate.

*For I, the L**ORD** your God,*

   hold your right hand;

it is I who say to you, "Do not fear,

   I will help you."

ISAIAH 41:13

I can't believe you want to punish me in such a horrible way, God. Surely you wouldn't be so cruel.

When I told my parents I was pregnant, they were very disappointed. A hurried wedding and a rocky financial start are not what they wanted for us. But we loved each other. Although some said the timing was not ideal, we rejoiced in this new child that would jump-start our real life together.

To have made it through the trauma and crisis and hurried arrangements, only to have the baby die so soon after the wedding seems too cruel. I don't understand, God. Help me to know what I am supposed to do next.

Hear my voice, LORD, when I call;

    have mercy on me and answer me.

PSALM 27:7 *(NAB)*

I keep thinking there must have been something I could have done to prevent this from happening — or something I shouldn't have done. Maybe I didn't eat the right foods or get enough exercise or rest. Maybe it was the wine I drank before I knew I was pregnant or the drinking I did back in college. Maybe I shouldn't have helped move the furniture at work that day. Maybe our vigorous lovemaking caused something to go wrong with the baby.

I wish I knew exactly what I did wrong. I don't want this to happen again.

Do nothing without deliberation,

    but when you have acted, do not regret it.

Do not go on a path full of hazards,

    and do not stumble at an obstacle twice.

SIRACH 32:19—20

*M*y neighbor died suddenly last week. She was fifty-three. I saw her mother at the funeral, and I could tell by her eyes that she feels like I do. The loss of a child is hard no matter when it comes, even when the child is a child no longer.

Do not fear death's decree for you;

    remember those who went before you and those

        who will come after.

This is the Lord's decree for all flesh.

SIRACH 41:3–4

I wanted to prove to everybody that this pregnancy wasn't going to turn me into a sissy. I had to show them I could still do everything I had done before. They teased me on the softball team, and I was determined to run just as fast and hit just as hard as I always had.

~ 70

The doctor doesn't know why I lost the baby, but he says it wasn't softball. I think my stupid pride killed my baby. How could the acceptance of a softball team have meant so much to me? I don't think I will be able to play softball for a very long time.

Again I saw that under the sun the race is not to the swift, nor the battle to the strong, nor bread to the wise, nor riches to the intelligent, nor favor to the skillful; but time and chance happen to them all.

ECCLESIASTES 9:11

My mother loves me very much, but she is clueless about miscarriage. I see the worry in her eyes. She thinks I should be getting over this by now, so I try to pretend, for her sake, that I am all right. I must not be very good at it, though, because she continues to worry.

I guess that's how it is with mothers; we love our children, and we worry. Why doesn't she understand that I still love my child, even though I never got to hold her? I worried about her and prayed for her, and I will always love her, just as my mother loves me.

Let your steadfast love become my comfort

according to your promise to your servant.

Let your mercy come to me, that I may live.

PSALM 119:76—77

73 ~

*S*o many babies. Mine
is not the only one. I know many mothers who
have lost a child, and I wonder why. Has it always
been this way? Is there something in our air
or water that is killing our babies? We know so
much about medicine, but this problem seems
to be getting bigger. Or maybe it just seems
bigger because I am part of it now.

So it is not the will of your Father in heaven that one of these little ones should be lost.

MATTHEW 18:14

*H*is life may have been short, but he was his own person. Before he was born, he used to wake up and kick every day at three o'clock. It was our special time. After he was born, he slept with his right hand beside his head, near the little lock of hair that always stuck up. He loved to have his back rubbed. He had a special look on his face when he saw me, and I know he recognized my voice. I remember how he smelled and the softness of his cheek. His little fingers clutched mine. He will always be with me in my heart.

His mother treasured all these things in her heart.

LUKE 2:51

*T*he women at work were complaining about their children today. One said she can't wait for school to start because the kids are driving her crazy. Another was worried because she doesn't like the guy her teenager is dating. She's tired of fighting with her daughter and wishes she would move out. Another was upset because her grown son is having money trouble again, and she's sure he will come to her for help.

Why do they seem so eager to be rid of their children? Don't they realize what a wonderful gift each moment they have with them is?

For where your treasure is, there your heart will be also.

LUKE 12:34

*T*hank you for the
gifts you have given me, Lord. Thank you for my
ability to love, even though it means pain. Thank
you for my strength. I didn't know I had it in
me. Thank you for my husband. He is my support.
Thank you for my faith. It gives me hope.

~ 80

But by the grace of God I am what I am,

and his grace toward me has not been in vain.

1 CORINTHIANS 15:10

~ REFLECTIONS

FOR FATHERS

*W*hat do you expect
of me, God? I can only handle so much. I am
not strong enough for this. I don't know how to
bear it.

~ 84

Is my strength the strength of stones,

or is my flesh bronze?

JOB 6:12

85 ~

*T*he ultrasound showed
no heartbeat. The baby is dead. Now we must wait
for contractions to begin. The doctor says they
will probably start in the next few days. How can
I endure it? A dead baby. Help me, Lord.

~ 86

I wait for the LORD, my soul waits,

    and in his word I hope;

my soul waits for the Lord

    more than those who watch for the morning.

I held her perfect little body. Tiny toes and fingers and wispy dark hair. It's hard to believe that just a few hours ago she was alive inside my wife. Something happened — I'm still not exactly sure what — and she died just before she was born. How could that precious little body be so lifeless?

~ 88

Holding her wasn't like I expected it to be, but I'm glad that at least I got to tell her that Daddy loves her.

. . . you are precious in my sight,

and honored, and I love you.

ISAIAH 43:4

*T*he nursery isn't ready.
The can of yellow paint is in the corner of the
room. The bolts for the crib are still in their little
plastic bag. The fish mobile is still in its box.
I didn't get it done in time, and now I have nothing but time. The baby is not coming home. She's
dead. Why didn't I finish the nursery sooner?
I don't know what to do now.

~ 90

He heals the brokenhearted,

and binds up their wounds.

PSALM 147:3

I feel so helpless, Lord. I am used to being able to find solutions, to fix things, to make them better. I can't fix this. I need you, God. What is my solution?

I cry aloud to God,

    aloud to God, that he may hear me.

In the day of my trouble I seek the Lord.

PSALM 77:1—2

*I*t's for the best," they say. "God wanted it that way."

They are trying to be comforting, but if their twenty-year-old son was killed by a car and I said, "It's for the best" or "God wanted it that way," I wonder if they would be comforted.

~ 94

"It's for the best," they say. "The baby was probably deformed." Do they think I could only love a perfect child?

They shall obtain joy and gladness,

and sorrow and sighing shall flee away.

I, I am he who comforts you.

ISAIAH 51:11—12

I'm afraid to talk about the baby because I don't want to bring up more pain for my wife. Still, our grief is palpable, and not to speak of it is like ignoring an elephant in the room. But the elephant doesn't go away if you talk about it — sometimes it seems only to grow larger. When will the elephant leave?

Blessed be the Lord,

    who daily bears us up;

    God is our salvation.

Our God is a God of salvation,

    and to GOD, the Lord, belongs escape from death.

97 ~

PSALM 68:19–20

I find if I throw myself into my work, it doesn't hurt as much. I've been getting a lot done at work since the baby died, but sometimes I just sit in my office and think of him. At times I cry a little, especially when I think of all the things we won't be able to do together or when I see my wife's sad face. I wish I could ease her pain. All I can do is hold her and let her hold me.

~ 98

It is an unhappy business that God has given to human beings to be busy with.

ECCLESIASTES 1:13

*I*t hurts to say, "My child is dead." It doesn't comfort or reassure me. It helps my wife to talk about our baby's death, but it only brings me pain. I don't want to talk about it — I can't. But I haven't forgotten anything.

~ 100

His memory is as sweet as honey to every mouth,

and like music at a banquet of wine.

SIRACH 49:1

I have never been the adventurous type, and change has always been hard for me. But this is the hardest change of all. I am different. I have lost my surety, and I know now that bad things can happen to me.

Help me, Lord, to grow with this change. I don't like it. I want to go back. I want everything to be good and happy again. Help me, Lord, to move forward.

Listen, I will tell you a mystery! We will not all die, but we will all be changed, in a moment, in the twinkling of an eye, at the last trumpet. For the trumpet will sound, and the dead will be raised imperishable, and we will be changed.

1 CORINTHIANS 15:51—52

Are they going to try again?" I heard my in-laws whisper as they talked about our miscarriage.

I've always resented it when people asked about our intentions with regard to having children. This time it took me by surprise. I have been so upset about the baby's death and so busy trying to comfort my wife that I hadn't thought about it. We have always wanted children, but it hurt so badly to lose this child. I don't know if we could stand the pain again.

God, give me faith and help me trust in you and your timing. Let my heart know that you won't give me or my wife more than we can bear. Help me believe that you have happiness in store for us.

If you have faith the size of a mustard seed,

you will say to this mountain, "Move from here

to there," and it will move; and nothing will

be impossible for you.

MATTHEW 17:20—21

I am ashamed to say that
I dread going home from work to my sad house.
It is so quiet. I look at my wife's face, and I see her
pain. I try to comfort her, but I don't know how.

~ 106

Husbands, in the same way, show consideration for your wives in your life together.

1 PETER 3:7

I feel buffeted by the wind. I thought I knew my life's path, at least for the next few months: our baby would be born, and we would be thrilled to have him or her. Everybody said the baby would change our lives completely, but it was a change we looked forward to embracing. This grief is so different from what we had planned. Our expectations were blown away.

The wind blows where it chooses, and you hear the sound of it, but you do not know where it comes from or where it goes. So it is with everyone who is born of the Spirit.

My father taught me to be strong and to protect my family. But I don't know how to protect them from this. I couldn't defend my baby from whatever it was that killed him. I can't protect my wife from her pain and from the knowledge that our baby is dead today and will be dead tomorrow and every day after that.

I love you, O LORD, my strength.

The LORD is my rock, my fortress, and my deliverer,

    my God, my rock in whom I take refuge,

    my shield, and the horn of my salvation,

      my stronghold.

                                  III ~

PSALM 18:1-2

FATHERS

I am a man. I am not a woman. Let me grieve as a man. I don't want to hug your sister or your mother. I don't want to talk about it. My baby is dead. I want to be left alone. I love you as you are. You are a woman. I am a man. Let me grieve as a man. Leave me alone for a while and let me grieve.

Woman is not independent of man or man independent of woman. For just as woman came from man, so man comes through woman; but all things come from God.

1 CORINTHIANS 11:11–12

113 ~

*G*od has always been my strength and support. Even as a young boy when things were bad in my family, I knew God loved me and cared for me. Later, I found a comfortable home in the Catholic church and a reassurance of the truth and wisdom to be found in its Scripture and tradition. I even seriously considered the seminary.

When we had our first miscarriage, I relied on God to get us through. Now another baby is dead, and I am angry. I haven't been able to go to Mass for six weeks. I can't understand. It is as if everything I thought was important and meaningful is now empty and hollow.

Why are you cast down, O my soul,

and why are you disquieted within me?

Hope in God; for I shall again praise him,

my help and my God.

PSALM 42:11

I wish I had done more
to keep this from happening. If I had come home
from work earlier, I could have fixed supper and
insisted that my wife sit down and relax. She was so
busy trying to wrap things up at work and get the
house ready for the baby. I wish I had been more

supportive and helpful. I don't know if it would
have made a difference, but I wish I had done more.

And forgive us our debts,

    as we also have forgiven our debtors.

MATTHEW 6:12

I thought I was a grown-up. I work and I take care of myself. I pay my bills on time. I love my wife. I take my responsibilities seriously and consider the consequences of my actions.

But the death of my son has shocked me into another kind of maturity. I know now how fragile life is and how essential it is that I do the important things — like tell my wife I love her and make time to play with the children.

Lay aside immaturity, and live,

and walk in the way of insight.

PROVERBS 9:6

I had so many hopes
and dreams for my child. They didn't seem like
unrealistic expectations.

May he grant you your heart's desire,
    and fulfill all your plans.

PSALM 20:4

*L*ord, do not let me
drown in my grief. Protect me from the fire
of my anger. Let not my sadness overwhelm me.

~ 122

When you pass through the waters, I will be
>   *with you;*
>   *and through the rivers, they shall not*
>   *overwhelm you;*
> *when you walk through fire you shall not be burned,*
>   *and the flame shall not consume you.*
> *For I am the L*ORD *your God.*

ISAIAH 43:2—3

We never dreamed
when we got married that this would be one
of the things we would have to endure together. I've
heard that adversity tears some couples apart and
makes others stronger. I don't know what this will
do to us; I only know that I need my darling's
love forever. I couldn't get through this without
my wife.

[Love] bears all things, believes all things, hopes all things, endures all things. Love never ends.

1 CORINTHIANS 13:7—8

I don't understand why my baby didn't live, God. I can't make sense of it. Someday I may understand, but for now I just want to get through this and live my life again.

But when I thought how to understand this,

it seemed to me a wearisome task,

until I went into the sanctuary of God;

then I perceived their end.

I don't have any ugly, hand-painted ties or a pencil holder made of a tin can. There are no pictures on my desk of grinning, snaggletoothed children, and I have nothing to add when the guys at work tell funny stories about their kids.

But I am a father. They don't know it, but I am. I hate that my baby died before I got to know her. I loved her and still do. No one at work knows about my little angel. I think of her smiling at me from heaven, and I talk to her sometimes. After all, I'm still her dad.

So you have pain now; but I will see you again,

and your hearts will rejoice, and no one will

take your joy from you.

JOHN 16:22

*W*e hold each other with tenderness. Our lovemaking means more now than ever. It represents everything our life together has become. It contains our joy and our sorrow, our delight and our passion. We support each other in this time of sadness. Even though our love-making is bittersweet, it nourishes us and helps us to go on. How I need you now, my precious love!

Sheepfolds and orchards bring flourishing health;

   but better than either, a devoted wife;

Wine and music delight the soul,

   but better than either, conjugal love.

SIRACH 40:19–20 *(NAB)*

~ REFLECTIONS

FOR MOTHERS

AND FATHERS

*T*he nurse smiled and held our hands. She was so gentle with the tiny little body, and she was kind as an angel. She prayed with us and swayed to the Alleluia. She tried to make it easier, but still it was hard.

~ 134

I am going to send an angel in front of you,

to guard you on the way and to bring you to

the place that I have prepared.

EXODUS 23:20

*N*ighttime is the worst.
I can stay busy during the day, but in the still of the
night my emptiness cannot be filled with busyness.

How I long to hold you, my little one. How
I long to kiss you and tell you how much I love
you. Why did God take you so soon? I miss you.

~ 136

I have been assigned months of misery,

    and troubled nights have been told off for me.

JOB 7:3 *(NAB)*

As I look back over
the recent past, I see only a blur of pain and
numbness. Am I alive or did I die with my baby?
I know part of me did. I think it was the happy
part. Will daylight ever come?

It is now the moment for you to wake from sleep.
For salvation is nearer to us now than when
we became believers; the night is far gone, the
day is near.

ROMANS 13:11—12

I am trying to make the best of this, Lord, but it is hard for me to understand the reason for this great loss. I can't see the good in it. Help me trust in you, Lord. I know you love me, but I need to tell you I'm feeling forgotten right now.

We know that all things work together for good for those who love God, who are called according to his purpose.

ROMANS 8:28

*W*hy do you ask this of me, God? I am unprepared. I have no experience losing someone I love. I am too young. I am not strong enough for this. I don't know what to do. I am not ready.

*But the L*ORD *said to me,*

*   "Do not say, 'I am only a boy';*

*   for you shall go to all to whom I send you,*

*   and you shall speak whatever I command you,*

*   Do not be afraid of them,*

*   for I am with you to deliver you, says the L*ORD*."*

JEREMIAH 1:7−8

143 ~

*T*here will be no night-time feedings. I won't have to get up in the middle of the night to tend to the baby. I used to worry about those feedings because I have always enjoyed my sleep. It's ironic — now that there is no baby to keep me awake, I can't sleep anyway.

O LORD, God of my salvation,

   when, at night, I cry out in your presence,

let my prayer come before you;

   incline your ear to my cry.

For my soul is full of troubles,

   and my life draws near to Sheol.

PSALM 88:1—3

I am exhausted. Sleep is a blessed relief, but I know I can't sleep all the time. I must try to live more fully. But I am so tired. Lord, give me your peace. Help me to truly rest so I won't be so tired. Heal me, Lord.

~ 146

He said, "My presence will go with you, and I will give you rest."

EXODUS 33:14

*T*he crib sits empty in the baby's room. She died in her sleep. I can't believe that my little girl is dead. My wife feels guilty because she was home and found her. But there was nothing she could have done.

I am afraid she thinks I blame her. I am heartbroken, and I fear that in addition to losing our darling daughter, we are losing each other. I don't know how to comfort my wife, and she doesn't know how to comfort me.

What can we do, Lord? How can an empty crib make us feel so alone?

Cast all your anxiety on him, because he cares for you.

1 PETER 5:7

*F*riends ask if I need anything. How can I tell them that what I really need is for my arms to be filled with my living, breathing son? I would never complain about sleepless nights or dirty diapers if only I could hold him, love him, and see him grow to manhood.

~ 150

If God so clothes the grass in the field that grows today and is thrown into the oven tomorrow, will he not much more provide for you, O you of little faith?

*I*s there a nursery in heaven where all the babies who died too soon are happy and playing and praising God? Does my baby know me and how much I want to hold her and nurture her? Is she waiting for me to come and play with her as I long to?

Let the little children come to me, and do not stop

them; for it is to such as these that the kingdom

of heaven belongs.

MATTHEW 19:14

*N*o one really knows how I feel. They think they do, and they try to understand. But there is only an emptiness filled with sadness.

You know me, God. You made me, and you gave me this caring heart. Please ease my pain.

My frame was not hidden from you,

when I was being made in secret,

intricately woven in the depths of the earth.

Your eyes beheld my unformed substance.

In your book were written

all the days that were formed for me,

when none of them as yet existed.

PSALM 139:15—16

*I*t's hard to endure
one day after another. They are not getting easier,
nor are they getting better. I still miss my child.
When will I be at peace?

~ 156

You need endurance to do the will of God and receive what he has promised.

HEBREWS 10:36 (*NAB*)

MOTHERS AND FATHERS

*O*ur baby was not perfect, but we loved her deeply. The ultrasound revealed severe malformations, and the doctor spoke gravely about pain. He said she had a strong heart and would probably live to term and perhaps a short time afterward. We knew our time together would be precious, so we treasured every moment we had with her. I'm glad she is no longer in pain, but I still miss her.

He will wipe every tear from their eyes.

Death will be no more;

mourning and crying and pain will be no more.

REVELATION 21:4

159 ~

*S*ome mornings I wake up feeling good. The sun is shining, the sheets are crisp. I stretch, and then I remember. How could I have forgotten? I won't see him or hold him today. I won't hear his voice or feel the touch of his soft skin.

Hear my words, O LORD;

listen to my sighing.

Hear my cry for help,

my king, my God!

To you I pray, O LORD;

at dawn you will hear my cry;

at dawn I will plead before you and wait.

PSALM 5:2–4 *(NAB)*

*M*y grief imprisons me. It clutches me with cold, steely fingers. The world is gray and lonely. Every action takes all my strength. I try to smile and act normally, especially around the people who love me and are concerned about me. I don't want them to worry — they are grieving too.

How will I ever move through this dark cloud? The days stretch endlessly before me, and I am so weary.

Bring me out of prison,

    so that I may give thanks to your name.

PSALM 142:7

*T*he path ahead of me
is long, and from here it seems empty. But I trust
you, Lord, to show me how to live each day.

~ 164

I will instruct you and teach you the way you

   should go;
I will counsel you with my eye upon you.

PSALM 32:8

~ 166

My eyes started to water during the opening song. Every phrase and prayer seemed to refer to our little baby. By the Gospel, tears streamed down my face. I left quietly during the Alleluia. By the time I got to the car, I was crying so hard I had to wait a few minutes before I could drive home. I've never walked out of Mass before, but it was too hard to hear those prayers and be surrounded by all those families.

Pour out your heart like water
before the presence of the Lord!
Lift your hands to him
for the lives of your children.

LAMENTATIONS 2:19

*Y*ou were once a tiny baby, Jesus. You know how my little one felt. She is gone, and although I didn't really get to know her, I miss her. Help me to know you, that I may come to find peace in her leaving.

~ 168

When I was born, I began to breathe the
    common air,
and fell upon the kindred earth;
my first sound was a cry, as is true of all.
I was nursed with care in swaddling cloths.
For no king has had a different beginning
    of existence;
there is for all one entrance into life, and one
    way out.

WISDOM 7:3-6

MICHAEL

I remember seeing the picture of little Michael when I was young. He was born twelve weeks prematurely and was so tiny that the wedding ring around his arm had plenty of room to spare. Still, he survived.

I kept thinking of him as I watched our little girl struggling for life. Like Michael, she too was born months early. But I was convinced she would live. After all, it has been twenty-five years since the book with little Michael's picture was written, and medical science has certainly advanced in that time. There is even a neonatology specialty now. Surely she would benefit from these strides. So how could it be that our little girl died?

Is there no balm in Gilead?

Is there no physician there?

JEREMIAH 8:22

I have countless blessings.
Many people love and support me. I have caring
family and friends, enough to eat, and a fine house.
I have my faith, and I know I am a beloved child
of God. I live in freedom with no real worries.
I have so much to be thankful for, and I am con-
stantly reminded of these blessings when I look
around at the brokenness in the world. I see people
whose families and countries are torn apart by
hatred, war, and famine. I am grateful; I did nothing to deserve being born into my circumstances.
I want to be content with all the blessings I have.

Be content with what you have; for he has said,

"I will never leave you or forsake you."

I don't know how to come to the end of this. It is as if my grief process has no aim or direction.

I know a funeral isn't an end to grief, but only the beginning. Yet at least it provides a real and symbolic end to the dying and a beginning to the time after death. It helps people to express their support and to acknowledge loss. The wake is a time to share memories and feelings. The deceased can be remembered with flowers and donations — it's all very concrete.

Without it, even death is nebulous. There is no body, no memorial, no Mass of the Resurrection, no acknowledgment of my child's life, much less his death. It's as if he never existed. But he did, and he does, and I want to scream the fact of his existence so he won't be forgotten in this world.

Do not avoid those who weep,

    but mourn with those who mourn.

SIRACH 7:34

When my baby died, I felt a rip in my soul. Although months have passed, the pain is still very real. I have to trust that God is slowly mending my spirit — first with basting threads and then with a beautiful stitch. But I wish he would sew me up quickly so the pain will stop. I know that the grief process is an important part of healing and that it must not be rushed. I do want to heal, but I don't want to do the work of grief. I just want it to be over.

Help me understand, Lord, that if I hurry you, it will be as if an unskilled apprentice sewed up my wound with uneven stitches that will not hold. If I allow you time to heal me, you will sew a fine seam and weave its pattern into the tapestry of my life, making it more beautiful than it was.

Then they cried to the LORD in their trouble,
and he saved them from their distress;
he sent out his word and healed them,
and delivered them from destruction.

*I*t is God's will," people say.
I just can't reconcile that statement with a
baby's death. They don't go together. God wills
life, sunshine, and gentle breezes. God wills majes-
tic mountains and fields of wildflowers. God wills
satisfying sex and melodious music. God wills
family harmony and joyous celebration. God wills
exuberant praise, abundant thanksgiving, and
heartfelt petition. God does not will death, destruction, and disease.

*I came that they may have life, and have
it abundantly.*

JOHN 10:10

179 ~

*G*od, you have known me all my life, even longer than I have known myself. As it turns out, I don't know myself as well as I thought I did. I don't seem to be handling this very well. I thought I would do better in a time of trial. I have faith in you, but I am still afraid. I am unsure of everything now. Help me, Lord, to trust in you.

~ 180

Do not fear, for I have redeemed you;

    I have called you by name, you are mine.

ISAIAH 43:1

*W*e are learning more than we ever wanted to know about cement vaults and caskets, health regulations and cremation. The decisions are hard and the solutions costly to dispose of the tiny shell that was my child. Yet they are important for those of us who remain.

Teach them the statutes and instructions and make known to them the way they are to go and the things they are to do.

EXODUS 18:20

So many people came to
the memorial service. It was all a little overwhelming. Family came from out of town as well as
friends I did not expect to see. They were there
to show their concern and love for us. It helps
to be reminded of how much people love and care
for us. And we still have each other.

Do not fear, for I am with you;

I will bring your offspring from the east,

and from the west I will gather you;

I will say to the north, "Give them up,"

and to the south, "Do not withhold;

bring my sons from far away

and my daughters from the end of the earth."

ISAIAH 43:5—6

MOTHERS AND FATHERS

γes, I am angry. How could you take my baby from me? You know how I loved him and longed for him.

~ 186

Be angry but do not sin; do not let the sun go down

on your anger, and do not make room for the devil.

EPHESIANS 4:26—27

Maybe it would be better if there had been a funeral — at least people would know our baby had died. Maybe then they would pretend to care.

Many of our friends act as if the miscarriage were simply something mildly sad that happened to someone far away. When we tell them what happened, they arrange their faces into what they hope will be an appropriately sad expression, offer the briefest of condolences, and then move on to a more interesting topic as quickly as possible. The next time they see us, they have clearly forgotten all about it and assume we have too. After all, they seem to think, it's not as if it were a real baby that we had gotten attached to.

My soul is bereft of peace;

I have forgotten what happiness is;

so I say, "Gone is my glory,

and all that I had hoped for from the LORD."

LAMENTATIONS 3:17–18

*I*t was like the lights went out for five years," I once heard someone say as they spoke of the death of a loved one.

I know now what they meant. This is like groping in darkness. I feel my whole life has changed. I am unsure of everything — from the meaning of my own existence to how I will manage to eat supper tonight. I only hope this darkness doesn't last for five years. I don't know how long it takes to get over something like this, but I know I am nowhere close. I also know I have been forever changed by it.

I hope that when the lights come back on, I'll see this change was for the better, although I don't know how it could be.

I will give you treasures out of the darkness,

and riches that have been hidden away,

That you may know that I am the LORD,

the God of Israel, who calls you by your name.

ISAIAH 45:3 *(NAB)*

*S*o few things remain
to show he existed: his little hat, the shirt he wore
so briefly, the "It's a Boy" card with his name,
birth date and weight that was attached to his iso-
lette, his tiny wristband, his footprints, and his
birth certificate. They all fit into a single envelope,
but signify the reality of our baby's short life on
this earth.

Are not two sparrows sold for a penny?
Yet not one of them will fall to the ground
apart from your Father.

MATTHEW 10:29

*T*hey try to show how sorry they are. Some bring casseroles, others look at their shoes and mumble. "Let us know what we can do," they say and really mean it.

But this death scares them and makes them uncomfortable. I feel sorry for their discomfort, but I am jealous because they get to go home and hug their children.

I want you to know how much I am struggling for you.

COLOSSIANS 2:1

*M*y baby was already
yours, God. Why couldn't he be mine for just
a little while longer?

~ 196

If we live, we live to the Lord, and if we die, we die to the Lord; so then, whether we live or whether we die, we are the Lord's.

ROMANS 14:8

MOTHERS AND FATHERS

*E*ven the church does
not acknowledge the existence of my daughter.
The church, which taught me to have "respect for
all human life from the moment of conception,"
does not provide a way to recognize her existence.
She didn't live long enough to be baptized, and
there was no pastoral visitation, no notation in the
parish archive, no Mass of the Resurrection, no
prayers of the faithful, no rite, no ritual, no symbol
in this liturgically rich tradition.

I don't know what I expect, or even what
I want, but there should be some way to say in
a public and communal way that we rejoice in the
very existence of our baby, that we grieve because
she is dead, and that we look forward to being
reunited with her in heaven.

O send out your light and your truth;

   let them lead me;

let them bring me to your holy hill

   and to your dwelling.

Then I will go to the altar of God,

   to God my exceeding joy;

and I will praise you with the harp,

   O God, my God.

PSALM 43:3—4

*W*e have so little time with the ones we love. We must make the most of this time together, and we must care for each other. In our mutual loss, may we find a closer bond to one another.

~ 200

When Jesus saw his mother and the disciple
whom he loved standing beside her, he said to his
mother, "Woman, here is your son." Then he said
to the disciple, "Here is your mother." And from
that hour the disciple took her into his own home.

JOHN 19:26—27

MOTHERS AND FATHERS

I am not functioning very well. Living with the knowledge that the baby is dead is painful. I feel so far away from you, God. I can only try to believe that you are sustaining me and guiding me through this. Please continue to stand by my side.

~ 202

If I take the wings of the morning
    and settle at the farthest limits of the sea,
even there your hand shall lead me,
    and your right hand shall hold me fast.

PSALM 139:9—10

*T*he Christmas stockings are hung, including ones too small to hold even a candy cane. Last year, our two-year-old son, Joe, asked who they were for. Our oldest son, Ben, lovingly explained that they belonged to their baby brother and sister who are in heaven with Jesus. This Christmas, Joe pointed them out to all our guests and told them about his babies in heaven.

His innocent faith is so beautiful. He cries for babies he never knew, and he looks forward to seeing them in heaven. His faith keeps me alive.

~ 204

*Since many have undertaken to compile a narrative
of the events that have been fulfilled among us,
just as those who were eyewitnesses from the beginning and ministers of the word have handed
them down to us, I too have decided, after investi-
gating everything accurately anew, to write it down
in an orderly sequence for you, most excellent
Theophilus, so that you may realize the certainty
of the teachings you have received.*

LUKE 1:1–4 *(NAB)*

I slipped into church for a quiet prayer. It was empty, but I was not alone. I felt your peace, Lord, and the sun seemed to be shining more brightly when I came out.

~ 206

How lovely is your dwelling place,

O LORD of hosts!

PSALM 84:1

*H*e looked so vulnerable with all those tubes and wires connected to his frail body. I've read stories and seen pictures of sick babies like him, but the stories always had happy endings. There was always a miracle for those little fighters, and I believed that was how it would be for us too. I prayed that the medical machines and neonatal specialists would save our baby. Why didn't they?

The LORD is near to all who call on him,

to all who call on him in truth.

PSALM 145:18

*E*verybody thinks
I should be "getting over this" by now. How can
they? Obviously they don't know how horrible
this is. They seem to believe that because my babies
weren't born, they were somehow less than real.

But they were real to me. Not just an anticipation or a hope, but a *reality*. Real babies who I
love and miss. They are my children, and my arms
ache to hold them. No, I'll never be over this.

*Restore us to yourself, O L*ORD*, that we may*

be restored;

renew our days as of old.

LAMENTATIONS 5:21

*W*e went to a support group tonight for parents whose babies have died. At first I was apprehensive about going. I've never been a "support group" type of person, and I thought we wouldn't fit in. But they were kind, and they listened and understood.

Looking back on the meeting, I don't know why I feel a little better, but I do. I'm going to go again next month.

Do not, O L<small>ORD</small>, withhold

your mercy from me;

let your steadfast love and your faithfulness

keep me safe forever.

PSALM 40:11

*H*er life was so short that the only mark she made on this world was in our hearts. We will never see her smile or know the color of her hair. She didn't grow up to accomplish great things, and she died before she even had a name. But she is not forgotten. She is our daughter.

Like a ship that sails through the billowy water,

and when it has passed no trace can be found,

no track of its keel in the waves.

WISDOM 5:10

MOTHERS AND FATHERS

*A*bout a year ago, our
parish started a group for young married couples.
They are still deciding what direction to take
and what kind of ministry to provide. For now,
they meet once a month over a potluck dinner
and get to know one another.

We had been active in the group, but since
the baby died I haven't been able to bring myself
to go. There are so many happy families there, and
I just can't take all those smiling faces right now.

God is faithful; by him you were called into the fellowship. . . .

1 CORINTHIANS 1:9

MOTHERS AND FATHERS

*L*ife has changed completely, but somehow it goes on. We are surviving. We don't understand, but we plod along and living gets a little easier each day. God has not abandoned us; there are pockets of hope and moments of happiness every now and then. Perhaps they will become more frequent.

We are afflicted in every way, but not crushed;

perplexed, but not driven to despair; persecuted,

but not forsaken; struck down, but not destroyed.

2 CORINTHIANS 4:8—9

*P*eople have been so kind. I can see the sadness in their eyes as they offer to help. There is nothing they can do, but they promise to keep us in their prayers. It helps to know that they care so much. Thank you for the blessing of friends, Lord.

May your friends be like the sun as it rises in its might.

JUDGES 5:31

I read an article last week about a baby who survived an abortion. Her mother paid to have her killed, but she did not die. She was placed in foster care and eventually adopted. She suffered a few physical handicaps as a result of the abortion attempt and now gives pro-life talks all over the country. I'm glad she survived and can serve as living evidence that real human beings are killed in abortions.

I must admit, however, that I am a little resentful that our baby, who was loved and cared for by so many, did not survive. Are you listening, God?

Put away from you all bitterness and wrath

and anger and wrangling and slander, together

with all malice, and be kind to one another,

tenderhearted, forgiving one another, as God

in Christ has forgiven you.

EPHESIANS 4:31—32

I don't know when things started to change, but gradually I found myself smiling, then laughing, then wanting to be with people instead of dreading it. The terrible pain has lessened to a dull ache. I still have days full of tears, but they are less frequent now. I can truthfully say that I have many days of happiness and joy.

A time to weep, and a time to laugh;

a time to mourn, and a time to dance.

ECCLESIASTES 3:4

MOTHERS AND FATHERS

*I*t has been a while since my little one died, and I can now begin to look back on that time of intense grief as something that is past. My sorrow carved a well in my heart, a well that has increased my capacity for joy and goodness. I try to appreciate the good times more fully now and to enjoy the opportunities I have for fun and happiness. My well of sorrow is becoming a spring of joy.

Then your light shall break forth like the dawn,

and your healing shall spring up quickly.

ISAIAH 58:8

I picked up my Bible today and thumbed through it. I was surprised by how many passages spoke to my heart and seemed to apply to me right now. I found comfort, strength, and nourishment.

~ 228

I commend you to God and to that gracious word of his that can build you up and give you the inheritance among all who are consecrated.

ACTS 20:32 (*NAB*)

*S*uch a short little life. It wasn't long enough for anything. And yet, all of our lives are too short for those who love us.

~ 230

You have made my days a few handbreadths,

and my lifetime is as nothing in your sight.

Surely everyone stands as a mere breath.

PSALM 39:5

MOTHERS AND FATHERS

I don't know when it happened, but at some point I realized that thinking of the baby was no longer accompanied by that searing pain, or that dreadful weight, or that grapefruit-sized lump in my throat. I began to smile inside when I thought of her, happy in the knowledge of her eternal existence and the awareness that she is forever a part of my heart.

You have turned my mourning into dancing;

you have taken off my sackcloth

and clothed me with joy.

*S*ome people say it is a shame. Others even imply that it would have been better if the baby had never been created. But the short time I had with my child is precious to me. It is painful now, but I still wouldn't wish it away. I prayed that God would bless us with a baby. Each child is a gift, and I am proud that we cooperated with God in the creation of a new soul for all eternity. Although not with me, my baby lives.

*For this child I prayed; and the L*ORD *has granted me the petition that I made to him.*

1 SAMUEL 1:27

I heard the birds today. They must have been singing every day for these past two months, but today I finally heard them. Maybe I am beginning to live again. I still feel pain and numbness, but I heard the birds today. Thank you, God, for their song.

For now the winter is past,

    the rain is over and gone.

The flowers appear on the earth;

    the time of singing has come,

and the voice of the turtledove

    is heard in our land.

SONG OF SOLOMON 2:11—12

MOTHERS AND FATHERS

*T*oday would have been
his birthday. I miss him so much. Help me to
celebrate today.

~ 238

Why is one day more important than another,

   when it is the sun that lights up every day?

SIRACH 33:7 *(NAB)*

MOTHERS AND FATHERS

*O*ur three-year-old
made a scrapbook in Sunday school today.
I was surprised to see two extra children in the
family portrait.

~ 240

As he showed me his book, he proudly
pointed out each person. When he came to the
extra children, he said, "These are my baby broth-
ers who died. They are in heaven now."

I was amazed. Those babies died before he
was born, and I had no idea that he would think to
include them when defining our family. I thought
I was the only one who remembers the babies
when we talk about who is in our family. It's funny
how we assume others don't think of our little
lost ones the way we do. I guess even though we
don't talk about it, we all remember.

*The steadfast love of the L*ORD *never ceases,*

his mercies never come to an end;

they are new every morning;

great is your faithfulness.

LAMENTATIONS 3:22—23

After a while the terrible pain begins to ease, and life becomes more normal. Missing the baby no longer brings that oppressive sadness; it simply becomes a part of everyday existence. Moments of hope and happiness become more frequent, and I can even be glad sometimes. I haven't forgotten. I still hold my baby in a special place in my heart, but now it is a happy place.

Let your father and mother be glad;

let her who bore you rejoice.

PROVERBS 23:25

*I*t has been some time now since our baby died, and although the anniversary of his death and birthday are still hard, I can honestly say that we have a happy life. Our family made it through this together, and we love each other more than ever. I can enjoy the beauty of the world around me and appreciate the many gifts God has given me.

I still miss my little darling, but I don't think about him all day, every day anymore. The overwhelming sadness is gone, and our days are filled with joy. We don't take our lives for granted now, and we try to make time for the things that are really important.

When our baby died, I wouldn't have thought it possible that I could ever be happy again.

I have said these things to you so that my joy may

be in you, and that your joy may be complete. This

is my commandment, that you love one another

as I have loved you.

The following are support organizations for bereaved parents. Many have chapters around the country to help you. You can find out more by contacting the offices listed below.

Bereaved Parents of the USA (BPUSA)
National Headquarters
P.O. Box 95
Park Forest, IL 60466
(708) 748-7672

Bereavement Services/RTS
1910 South Avenue
LaCrosse, WI 54601
(608) 791-4747
(800) 362-9567 ext. 4747

Center for Loss in Multiple Birth (CLIMB)
P.O. Box 1064
Palmer, AK 99645
(907) 746-6123

The Compassionate Friends (TCF)
National Office
P.O. Box 3696
Oak Brook, IL 60522-3696
(708) 990-0010

National SIDS Foundation
1314 Bedford Avenue
Suite 210
Baltimore, MD 21208
(410) 653-8226
(800) 221-7437

Pen-Parents
P.O. Box 8738
Reno, NV 89507-8738
(702) 826-7332

Pregnancy and Infant Loss Center (PILC)
1421 East Wayzata Boulevard
Suite 30
Wayzata, MN 55391
(612) 473-9372

Resolve, Inc.
(for infertility)
National Office
1310 Broadway
Somerville, MA 02144-1731
(617) 623-0744

Share Pregnancy & Infant Loss Support, Inc.
National Office
St. Joseph Health Center
300 First Capital Drive
St. Charles, MO 63301-2893
(800) 821-6819

Sidelines National Support Network
(for complicated pregnancies)
P.O. Box 1808
Laguna Beach, CA 92652
(717) 497-2265

Chris Lafser makes her home in Virginia with her husband, Bill, and their two sons, Ben and Joseph. Having lost two children to death, she has helped many other grieving parents.